THE TRUE STORY OF THE HARLEM HELLFIGHTERS IN WORLD WAR I

by Emmett J. Scott

Editor's Note: The text of this volume, first published in 1919, contains terms that may be considered offensive by today's standards; however, for the sake of authenticity, the original language has been preserved.

AUTHOR'S PREFACE

The Negro, in the great World War for Freedom and Democracy, has proved to be a notable and inspiring figure. The record and achievements of this racial group, as brave soldiers and loyal citizens, furnish one of the brightest chapters in American history. The ready response of Negro draftees to the Selective Service calls—together with the numerous patriotic activities of Negroes generally, gave ample evidence of their whole-souled support and their 100 percent Americanism. It is difficult to indicate which rendered the greater service to their Country—the 400,000 or more of them who entered active military service (many of whom fearlessly and victoriously fought upon the battlefields of France) or the millions of other loyal members of this race whose useful industry in fields, factories, forests, mines, together with many other indispensable civilian activities, so vitally helped the Federal authorities in carrying the war to a successful conclusion.

When war against Germany was declared April 6, 1917, Negro Americans quickly recognized the fact that *it was not to be a white man's war, nor a black man's war, but a war of all the people living wider the "Stars and Stripes" for the preservation of human liberty throughout the world.* Despite efforts of pro-German propagandists to dampen their ardor or cool their patriotism by pointing out seeming inconsistencies between their treatment as American citizens and their expected loyalty as American soldiers, more than one million of them (1,078,331), according to the Second Official Report of the Provost Marshal General, promptly responded to, and registered under the three Selective Service calls. More than 400,000 Negro soldiers (367,710 draftees plus voluntary enlistments and those already in the Regular Army) were called to the colors and offered their lives in defense of the American flag during the recent war. Relative to their population, proportionately more Negroes were "drafted" than was true of white men.

The Negro was represented in practically every branch of military service during the Great World War—including Infantry, Cavalry, Engineer Corps, Field Artillery, Coast Artillery, Signal Corps (radio or wireless telegraphers), Medical Corps, Hospital and Ambulance Corps, Aviation Corps (ground section), Veterinary Corps, and in Stevedore Regiments, Service or Labor Battalions, Depot Brigades, and so forth.

Nor was this the first instance in the Nation's history that this ever-loyal racial group rightly and cheerfully responded to the tocsin of war and made a military record of which any race might well be proud. In the Revolutionary War, in the War of 1812, in the Mexican War, in the Civil War, and in the War with Spain, the American Negro soldier has always distinguished himself by bravery, fortitude, and loyalty. His military record has always compared favorably with that of other soldiers.

THE TRUE STORY OF THE HARLEM
HELLFIGHTERS IN WORLD WAR I

The first effort to organize a colored National Guard regiment in New York City was sponsored by Charles W. Fillmore, a colored citizen, who afterwards was commissioned a Captain in the "15th" [the 15th New York National Guard Regiment, which afterwards became the 369th Infantry—the "Harlem Hellfighters"—prior to its going overseas] by Col. William Hayward. The effort to secure proper approval of such a regiment was more or less abortive until Gov. Charles S. Whitman, following the gallant fight of Negro troops of the Tenth Cavalry against Mexican bandits at Carrizal, authorized the project and named Col. Hayward, then Public Service Commissioner, to supervise the task of recruiting an organization. It was found that there were more than two hundred Negro residents of the city who had seen service in the regular army, or in the militia of other states. With these as a nucleus the work of recruiting began on June 29, 1916.

By the first of October, ten companies of sixty-five men each had been formed, and the regiment was then recognized by the State and given its colors. By April 8, 1917, the regiment had reached peace strength, with 1,378 men, and was recognized by the Federal Government. Two weeks later the organization was authorized to recruit to war strength. The 600 men needed were recruited in five days after the applicants had been subjected to a physical examination more stringent than that given in the regular army. The first battalion of four companies was recruited in Manhattan, the second battalion was composed of Brooklyn men, and the third of men from Manhattan and the Bronx. "There is no better soldier material in the world," said Col. Hayward, following the organization of the regiment. "Given the proper training, these men will be the equal of any soldiers in the world."

Training the Regiment

Training the men presented some difficulty. At first they were drilled in Lafayette Hall, 132nd Street and Seventh Avenue, New York City. But the place was altogether too small and many of the fifty squads which drilled nightly had to take to the streets to carry out the maneuvers of their drill sergeants. Later they went for three weeks to Camp Whitman [near Poughkeepsie, N.Y.]. An announced plan to send the regiment to train at Camp Wadsworth, Spartanburg,

S.C., caused a storm of protest from the citizens of the South Carolina town.

"The most tragic consequences," they insisted, "would follow the introduction of the New York Negro with his Northern ideas into the community life of Spartanburg." The Spartanburg Chamber of Commerce drafted resolutions protesting against the training of Negro troops at Camp Wadsworth, which were sent to New York State officials. The resolutions, however, had less weight than the exigencies of war and, early in October, the 15th Negro Infantry detrained at Camp Wadsworth. The "tragic consequences" did not materialize. Certain stores refused to serve Negro customers and were, in turn, boycotted by the white soldiers, but the chief result of the Fifteenth's visit to Spartanburg was an increased respect in some measure, at least, for the black soldier.

While at Spartanburg the regiment was supplied with the latest things in trench shoes, heavy underwear, and other overseas supplies. This led the men to expect immediate transfer overseas. They were, indeed, ordered overseas, but the regiment made three distinct starts for France before it finally got away from America. The accident that caused the first turning back occurred when still in sight of the Narrows. The vessel was disabled by a bent piston rod and had to put back to the Brooklyn Navy Yard for repairs. Four days later the ship put out again, only to halt when fire was found in the reserve coal bunker. Putting back to Hoboken, the sorely tried Fifteenth counted the hours until a new transport could be obtained. Hours became days, and days weeks, but still no other ship offered.

Delayed by Storm and Collision

Finally, on December 3, 1917, the Navy Department notified the transport's commander to put to sea. But while the pier lines were being cast off, a storm started to blow up, and by the time the *Pocahontas*—nameless at the time—reached the outer bay, the greatest blizzard of the year was raging. Clouds of snow, through which nothing could be seen, forced the *Pocahontas* to drop anchor. She had hardly done so when a huge hulk, appearing suddenly through the murk, bore down upon the transport's bow and cut a ten-foot hole in her side. Then the storm abated in the bay, but a new one arose below decks, where 3,000-odd exasperated soldiers were maintaining their belief that no such place as France existed. The captain of the transport was for turning back again to the Navy Yard. The hole was above the waterline, he admitted, and there was no great danger impending as a result of the collision, he said. Nevertheless there would be an inquiry, and it was necessary that he be present to state his case.

"I can see no reason for turning back except that of fear," said Col. Hayward to the captain. The captain did not turn back. There was an ambulance assembly unit onboard with electric drills. Ten hours, it was said, would suffice to make sufficient repairs to enable the vessel to proceed. The bent plates were drilled out and double planking erected in their place. Concrete was then poured between the planks. The result was not elegant, but the ship was watertight and, best of all, still bound for France.

Brest [in northwestern France] was reached on December 27 without incident except for an epidemic of German measles, which attacked the crew of the transport, but which was escaped by nearly all officers and men of the Fifteenth.

From Brest the regiment was transferred to St. Nazaire, where the troops were put to work constructing a huge railroad yard, building roads, and unloading ships. The fact of being in the country "where the war is" helped the impatient soldiers to endure their lot for a while, but before long there was a general feeling that "while stevedoring may be all right, it is not war," and the officers were besieged with apologetic and respectful queries: "When do we fight?"

Guarding German Prisoners

The answer was assumed to have been supplied when, early in January, the Third Battalion was ordered to Colquidan, in Brittany [region of northwestern France], where there was a big American artillery camp. It turned out, however, that peace was still longer to bear down upon the spirits of the Fifteenth. At Colquidan, they found, as well as an American artillery camp, there was also a large German prison camp, and it was for the purpose of guarding this camp that their services were required.

Three weeks passed, and then the Third Battalion received orders to join the rest of the regiment at Givry-en-Argonne [in northeastern France], there to be formally transferred to the French high command and to be known as the 369th Regiment d'Infanterie Etats Unis (United States Infantry). Actual fighting was still far off, it seemed to the soldiers, for they were put to training under French officers. One hundred and twenty picked men and a number of officers were sent to the French Divisional Training School, where they were taught to use the French arms, including grenades, French bayonets, rifles and machine guns. Upon the completion of the course, others of the former Fifteenth were sent to take this training.

They proved apt pupils. In grenade-throwing they easily outdid their instructors, and in bayonet work they demonstrated great skill. They surprised the French, also, with the manner in which they acquired the French language. Many of them were talking quite fluently after a week with their French comrades. It turned out, however, that many of the soldiers hailed from Louisiana, and that their new environment merely had revived forgotten memories of the French language.

In May the regiment went to the Main de Massiges, a part of the French line which offered the greatest danger as well as the greatest opportunity for training in trench warfare and raiding. A small number of the Fifteenth's men were sent with each French company, with instructions to observe all regulations and familiarize themselves with the tactics of the French. The French *poilus* [infantry soldiers] were delighted with their colored comrades and soon sought to teach them all they knew.

After two weeks' experience obtained in the manner described, the 369th was sent into action in the Bois d'Hauze, Champagne [in northeastern France], where the regiment, unassisted by the French, held a complete sector, which in length constituted 20 percent of all territory held by American troops at the time. In this action, which lasted until July 4, 1918, when the colored soldiers, their ranks thinned by the deadly German fire and completely worn out, were relieved by the 4th French *Chasseurs-à-pied* [soldiers fighting on foot].

Fighting Ability Recognized

By this time the fighting effectiveness of the Negro troops from New York was recognized by the high command, and after resting behind the lines for a few weeks they were transferred and placed in the path of the expected German offensive at Minancourt, near Butte de Mesnil, where they bore the brunt of the German attacks of July 15 and thereafter. Against the enemy in this action the old Fifteenth was completely successful, holding against the German fire, repelling German attacks, and by counter-attacks becoming possessed of the front-line German trenches.

At the end of July the regiment, after a three days' march to the rear, went into training for open warfare, but had hardly started work when a hurry call was sent to them to take over the same place in the line which they had left a few days before. Motor lorries [trucks] were impressed [put into service] and the New York soldiers hastened back to the front, arriving in time to assist in repelling the most violent German attacks.

During the action which followed, it was the policy of the French strategists to retreat from the lines then held, after having "gassed" all the dug-outs. The advancing Germans thereupon were met with such heavy shellfire that they were forced into the underground shelters and so fell by the hundreds, victims of the noxious fumes released by the French.

The men of the 369th, advancing again after this defeat of the enemy, found enough Mauser rifles lying beside the dead Germans to equip an entire brigade. Finding the German Mauser to resemble the Springfield formerly used by the American troops and preferring it to the French weapon furnished them, the men of the Fifteenth promptly adopted the captured rifle, and it was with considerable difficulty that the French equipment was finally restored to them.

Wins the Croix de Guerre

Early in September the men of the 369th were transferred from the 16th French Division, in which they had been serving, and made an integral part of the 161st French Division. And then, on the morning of September 26, they joined with the Moroccans on the left and native French on the right in the offensive which won for the entire regiment the French Croix de Guerre [a military decoration; Cross of War] and the citation of 171 individual officers and enlisted men for the Croix de Guerre and the Legion of Honor, for exceptional gallantry in action. The action began at Maison-en-Champagne; it finished seven kilometers northward and eastward and over the intervening territory the Germans had retreated before the ferocious attacks of the Fifteenth and its French comrades.

A month later a new honor came to the regiment—the honor of being the first unit of all the Allied armies to reach the River Rhine. The regiment had left its trenches at Thann, Sunday, November 17, and, marching as the advance guard of the 161st Division, Second French Army, reached Blodelsheim, on the left bank of the Rhine, Monday, November 18. The 369th is proud of this achievement. It believes also that it was under fire for a greater number of days than any other American regiment. Its historian will record:

That the regiment never lost a man captured, a trench, or a foot of ground; that it was the only unit in the American Expeditionary Force which bore a State name and carried a State flag; that it was never in an American brigade or division; that it saw the first and the longest service of any American regiment as part of a foreign army; and that it had less training than any American unit before going into action.

Letter from Colonel Hayward

A highly significant letter written by Col. Hayward to the author [Emmett J. Scott] shortly after the 369th reached France and went into training may be quoted:

Dear Scott:

Am writing this from away up on the French front where the "Fighting Fifteenth," now the 369th U.S., is really fighting in a French Division. We are known to the French as 369 R.I.M.S. and our *Secteur Postal* is No. 54, France.

I have two battalions in the trenches of the *first* line and the third in relief at rest just behind our trenches. The three rotate. Our boys have had their baptism of fire. They have patrolled No Man's Land. They have gone on raids and one of my lieutenants has been cited for a decoration. Of course, it is still in the experimental stage, but two questions of the gravest importance to our country and to your race have, in my opinion, been answered.

First: How will American Negro soldiers, including commissioned officers (of whom I still have five), get along in service with French soldiers and officers—as for instance a Negro regiment of infantry serving in a French combat division?

Second: Will the American Negro stand up under

the terrible shell fire of this war as he has always stood under rifle fire and thus prove his superiority, spiritually and intellectually, to all the black men of Africa and Asia, who have failed under these conditions and whose use must be limited to attack or for shock troops?

We have answered the first question in a most gratifying way. The French soldiers have not the slightest prejudice or feeling. The *poilus* and my boys are great chums, eat, dance, sing, march and fight together in absolute accord. The French officers have *little*, if any feeling about Negro officers. What little, if any, is not racial but from skepticism that a colored man (judging of course by those they have known) can have the technical education necessary to make an efficient officer. However, as I write these lines, Capt. Napoleon Bonaparte Marshall and Lieut. D. Lincoln Reed are living at the French Officers' Mess at our division *Infanterie* School, honored guests.

The program I enclose gives you an idea of the way I've cultivated friendship between my boys and the *poilus*. You should have seen the 500 soldiers, French and mine, all mixed up together, cheering and laughing at the show arranged while the Boche shells (boxcar size) went screaming over our heads.

Now, on the second question, perhaps I am premature. But both my two battalions which have gone in have been under shellfire, serious and prolonged once, and the boys just laughed and cuddled into their shelter and read old newspapers. French company got shelled and it was getting very warm around the rolling kitchen. The cooks went along about their business in absolute unconcern until the alarmed French soldiers ran to them and told them to beat it. One of the cooks said, "Oh, that's all right, boss. They ain't hurting us none." They are positively the most stoical and mysterious men I've ever known. Nothing surprises them. And we now have expert opinion. The French officers say they are entirely different from their own African troops and the Indian troops of the British, who are so excitable under shellfire. Of course, I have explained that my boys are public school boys, wise in their day and generation, no caste prejudice, accustomed to the terrible noises of the subway, elevated and street traffic of New York City (which would drive any desert man or Himalaya mountaineer mad) and are all Christians. Also, that while the more ignorant ones might not like to have a black cat hanging around for fear it would turn into a fish or something, they have no delusions about the Boche shells coming from any Heathen Gods. They know the d—— child-killing Germans are firing at them with pyrocellulose and they know how the breech mechanism works.

I am very proud of what we've done and are doing. I put the whole regiment through grenade (live grenade) practice. Nasty, dangerous business. They did it beautifully. I found one rank arrant coward, who refused to throw. Said he couldn't. Another threw prematurely after igniting the bomb. We asked him why he did not wait for the command to throw (barrage). He said, "Kunnel, that old grenade, she begun to swell right in my hand." The boys keep writing home that the "war is not so bad if you just go at it right." Well, a very wise command somewhere, I don't know where, has let us go at it right. You know I've always told these boys I'd never send them anywhere I would not go myself, so I went first to the trenches, prowled around, saw it all and came back to the regiment to take in the battalion which was to go in first. When they saw me covered with mud, but safe and sound, they said, "How is she, Kunnel?" "She's all right," I said. They all laughed and then the sick and the lame of that battalion began to get well miraculously and begged to go. Captain Clark called for twelve volunteers for a raid and the company fell in to the last man—all wanted to go, and he had to pick his twelve after all.

Do you wonder that I love them, every one, good, bad and indifferent?

Personally I am well, strong, and the happiest man in the world. I've learned more about the military game, at least the fighting of this war, since I have been here with the French than I learned in all the years as drummer boy, private, Sergeant, Captain, Major and Colonel Second Nebraska Infantry, Spanish War, Maneuvers, Officers' School, Gettysburg and Leavenworth problems, etc., etc., and all the time I spent with my present regiment in the New York National Guard.

And another thing, I believe I know more about Negro soldiers and how to handle them, especially the problem of Negro and white officers, than any other man living today. Of course, the other regiment I commanded for three years was a white regiment, so I had a lot to learn, but I've learned it and I wouldn't trade back now.

Suppose after I've held my sector up here by blood and iron two or three months, some National Guard Brigadier, who has just arrived in France, will come along and point out all the mistakes I've made and tell me just how to do it. Well, *"C'est la guerre,"* as we French say.

Brother Boche doesn't know who we are yet, as none of my men have been captured so far, and the boys wear a French blue uniform when they go on raids. I've been thinking if they capture one of my Puerto Ricans (of whom I have a few) in the uniform of a Normandy French regiment and this black man tells them in Spanish that he is an American soldier in a New York National Guard regiment, it's going to give the German intelligence department a headache trying to figure it out.

We are proud to think our boys were the first Negro American soldiers in the trenches. Jim Europe was certainly the first Negro officer in. You can imagine how important he feels! In addition to the personal gratification at having done well as a regiment I feel it has been a tremendously important experiment, when one considers the hosts of colored men who must come after us. I wish I had a brigade, yes, a division or a corps of them. We'd make history and plant the hob-nailed boots of the "Heavy Ethiopian Foot" in the Kaiser's face all right.

We were so disappointed that the Secretary didn't get up to see us. The town we were holding then had been named by me "Bakerville" and it is so on our maps.

Regards and good wishes to you.

Sincerely,

William Hayward

Called "Hell Fighters" by the Enemy

The men of the 369th came to be known among the French and the Germans as "Hell Fighters." The regiment participated in the action which followed the German offensive on the 15th of July, 1918, when the Germans were reinforced by released prisoners from Russia, so that they then had their maximum forces. They had broken through the British line and disaster was at hand. This was east of Rheims. The Germans had also torn through the French at Montdidier and had gone through for 30 or 40 kilometers.

During the 191 days that the regiment was in the trenches there were weeks in that immediate sector when there was nothing between the German army and Paris but these black men from America. It was through the action of the men of the 369th in capturing German prisoners on the night of July 14 that the expected German attack was learned. When the

French found out that the great German offensive was coming, their forces did not remain a thin blue line. Gen. Gouraud, who commanded the Fourth French Army, took his troops out of the front line trenches over a front of 50 kilometers, and when the attack occurred he had the 369th on one flank of a 50-kilometer line and the old 69th New York, a part of the Rainbow Division, on the other. When the German fire fell on these front-line trenches for five hours and twenty minutes, the shells fell on empty trenches except for a few patrols left in reinforced trenches with signal rockets, gas shells, and a few machine guns. When the hour for the German infantry attack came, these patrols let off their gas bombs and signal rockets and the massed allied artillery let loose on the massed Germans, who were literally smashed and never got through to the second line of the 369th. On the other end they did get through, crashing into the Rainbow Division and the old 69th New York, which met them hand-to-hand in some of the most terrible fighting of the war.

Individual Exploits of the 369th

There are many outstanding exploits of the men of the 369th and of Col. Hayward himself. In Belleau Wood on June 6, 1918, the regiment came up to the German front lines where it met a very heavy counterattack. Someone suggested that they turn back. "Turn back? I should say we won't. We are going through there or we don't come back," was what

Colonel Hayward said as he tore off the eagles of his insignia, grabbed a gun from a soldier, and darted out ahead of the rest of Company "K," which went through a barrage of German artillery that was bearing down upon it. A French General ordered the regiment to retire, but Colonel Hayward, who, of course, was under direct command of this French General said: "I do not understand you."

Then the French General raised his arms above his head and cried:

"Retire! Retire!"

And then Colonel Hayward, with his hat knocked off, came running up and cried: "My men never retire. They go forward, or they die!"

A Prussian officer captured by the "Black Watch," as the 369th was called after they had reached the Rhine, is said to have remarked: "We can't hold up against these men. They are devils! They smile while they kill and they won't be taken alive."

The regiment was eleven times cited for bravery in action, and Colonel Hayward himself received a citation, reading: "Colonel Hayward, though wounded, insisted on leading his regiment in battle."

A typical story of the daredevil courage of the men of the 369th is afforded in the exploit of Elmer McCowin of Company "K," who won the Distinguished Service Cross. He tells his own story as follows: "On September 26 the Captain asked me to carry dispatches. The Germans pumped machine gun bullets at me all the way. But I made the trip and back safely. Then I was sent out again. As I started with the message, the Captain yelled to bring him back a can of coffee. He was joking, but I didn't know it at the time.

"Being a foot messenger, I had some time ducking those German bullets. Those bullets seemed very sociable, but I didn't care to meet up with them, so I kept right on traveling on high gear. None touched my skin, though some skinned pretty close.

"On the way back it seemed the whole war was turned on me. One bullet passed through my trousers and it made me hop, step, and jump pretty lively. I saw a shell hole six feet deep. Take it from me, I dented another six feet when I plunged into it hard. In my fist I held the Captain's can of coffee.

"When I climbed out of the shell hole and started running again, a bullet clipped a hole in the can and the coffee started to spill. But I turned around, stopped a second, looked the Kaiser in the face, and held up the can of coffee with my finger plugging up the hole to show the Germans they were fooled. Just then another bullet hit the can and another finger had to act as a stopgap.

"It must have been good luck that saved my life, because bullets were picking at my clothes and so many hit the can that at the end all my fingers were hugging it to keep the coffee in. I jumped into shell holes, wriggled along the ground, and got back safely. And what do you think? When I got back into our own trenches I stumbled and spilled the coffee!"

Not only did Lieut. George Miller, Battalion Adjutant, confirm the story, but he added about Private McCowin: "When that soldier came back with the coffee, his clothes were riddled with bullets. Yet half an hour later he went back into No-Man's-Land and brought back a number of wounded until he was badly gassed. Even then he refused to go to the rear and went out again for a wounded soldier. All this under fire. That's the reason he got the DSC [Distinguished Service Cross]."

Corporal Elmer Earl, also of Company "K," living at Middletown, New York, also won the Distinguished Service Cross. He explained: "We had taken a hill September 26 in the Argonne. We came to the edge of a swamp, when enemy machine guns opened fire. It was so bad that of the fifty-eight of us who went into a particular strip, only eight came out without being killed or wounded. I made a number of trips out there and brought back about a dozen wounded men."

How Sergeant Butler Won the Distinguished Service Cross

On authority of General Pershing, Colonel Hayward himself presented the Distinguished Service Crosses to the heroes among his regiment. Then, from the hands of General Collardet, of the French Army, he received the medal of the Legion of Honor. But even among this list of distinguished heroes, those who knew of the exploits of Sergeant "Bill"

Butler insisted upon calling for him and making him the object of their attentions.

It was on the night of August 12, 1918, while the fighting was raging in the Champagne district, that Sergeant Butler's opportunity came to him. A German raiding party had rushed the American trenches and, after firing a few shots and making murderous use of the short trench knives and clubs carried for such encounters, had captured five privates and a lieutenant. The victorious raiders were making their way back to their own trenches when Butler, occupying a lone position in a forward post, saw that it would be necessary for the party to pass him.

The Negro sergeant waited until the Germans were close to his post, then opened fire upon them with his automatic rifle. He kept the stream of lead upon the raiders until ten of their number had been killed. Then he went forth and took the German lieutenant—who was slightly wounded—a prisoner, released the American lieutenant and five other prisoners, and returned to the American lines with his prisoner and the rescued party.

Under the heading "Trenton Has Nothing on Salisbury," *The Afro-American* of Baltimore said: "Trenton, New Jersey, may have her Needham Roberts, but it takes Salisbury, Maryland, to produce a William Butler. Roberts had his comrade, Henry Johnson, to help him in repulsing a raiding party of Germans, but Butler took care of a German lieutenant and squad of Boches all by himself. Herbert

Corey, a white newspaper correspondent, in telling of the incident, said that Butler came 'a-roaring and fogging' through the darkness with his automatic, and 'nobody knows how many Germans he killed.' It was for this that General Pershing awarded him the Distinguished Service Cross recently and the citation read: 'Sergt. William Butler, Company L, 369th Infantry (A.S. No. 104464). For extraordinary heroism in action near Maison de Champagne, France, August 18, 1918. Sergeant Butler broke up a German raiding party which had succeeded in entering our trenches and capturing some of our men. With an automatic rifle he killed four of the raiding party and captured or put to flight the remainder of the invaders. Home address, Mrs. Jennie Butler, Water Street, Salisbury, Maryland.'

"The rest of the State of Maryland and the whole United States now has its hat off to Butler of Salisbury."

And the *New York Tribune,* on April 28, 1919, said: " 'Bill' Butler, a slight, good-natured colored youth, who until two years ago was a jack-of-all-trades in a little Maryland town, yesterday came into his own as a hero among heroes. More than 5,000 men and women arose to their feet in City College stadium and cheered themselves hoarse while representatives of two governments pinned their highest medals upon the breast of the nervous youth. Sergeant Butler was one of a list of twenty-three members of the famous 15th Regiment upon whom both France and the

United States conferred medals of honor because of extraordinary heroism on European battlefields. But by common consent his name comes first on the list—a list that was made up only after a careful comparison of the deeds of gallantry that finally resulted in the breaking of the Hun lines."

Won the Cheers of the French

Of the 369th it may be stated that although the Germans never captured a single man, they killed nearly 200 of them and wounded more than 800 others, but on the other side of the score were to be found more than 400 Germans captured by the Third Battalion of the 369th alone, and countless men of the enemy killed and wounded.

It proved itself to be one of the most efficient military units of all the Allied forces. The officers and men were constantly cheered by the gratitude of the French, who never failed to place in evidence their appreciation for the wonderful fighting prowess of the men of the 369th. The French were amazed not only at the proficiency of the men as soldiers but at their proficiency in laying railroad tracks, which was the first duty assigned them near one of the larger French ports. The 369th laid many stretches of track, pushed them into alignment, gave twists to the bolts, and proceeded half a mile farther down to repeat the performance. *"Magnifique!"* exclaimed a party of French officers who watched them do the work.

The story of the wanderings of "the old 15th," of

its hard fighting in France, of its returning to America, and of the triumphant procession through the streets of New York City, down Fifth Avenue, is one of the proudest possessions of the Negro race and of American arms.

Five colored officers went over with the 369th Regiment. These officers were afterwards transferred to the 92nd Division. Considerable criticism followed the transfer of these colored officers from a colored regiment which had won such renown as the 369th. Col. Hayward, however, gave the following as reason for the transfer:

"In August, 1918, the American Expeditionary Force adopted the policy of having either all white or all colored officers with Negro regiments, and so ours were shifted away (though Lieut. Europe later was returned to us as bandmaster, whereas he had been in the machine gun force before). Our colored officers were in the July fighting and did good work, and I felt then and feel now, that if colored officers are available and capable, they, and not white officers, should command colored troops. I hope, if the Fifteenth is reconstructed, as it should be, colored men will have the active work of officering it, from top to bottom.

"There is splendid material there. I sent away forty-two sergeants in France who were commissioned officers in other units. I would have sent others, but they declared they'd rather be sergeants in the Fifteenth than lieutenants or captains in other regiments."

CPSIA information can be obtained
at www.ICGtesting.com
Printed in the USA
LVHW080517150420
653530LV00018B/1870